DEPRESSION AND DAFFODILS

A Journey Through Darkness into Light

AVYNEET

First Edition: 2024
Cover Design by: Avyneet
Interior Design by: Avyneet
Illustrations by: Avyneet

Published by: Bhavneet Kaur (Avyneet)

This book is dedicated to all those who find hope blooming in unexpected places.

DEDICATION

For my grandmother— whose love taught me that flowers can grow even in the hardest seasons. You planted hope in my soil when I had nothing but shadows, and your strength still blooms in everything I write. In every daffodil that breaks through winter's ground, I see your gentle smile.

And for every soul who believed in me— when I lost sight of my own light, you became my horizon. When my garden turned to wilderness, you stayed to watch the flowers grow. Your faith in me became the sunlight that helped my words bloom.

This garden of poems grows in your honor, each page a petal opening toward the light you helped me find.

"Sometimes it takes a whole garden to help one flower believe in spring."

AUTHOR'S NOTE

Dear Reader, This book was born in the spaces between darkness and dawn, in those quiet moments when pain and hope dance together like shadows and light. Each poem is a piece of a journey —from the depths where depression threatened to root , to the moments when hope first pushed through like stubborn daffodils in winter soil.

Some of these pages might feel heavy; they carry the weight of sleepless nights and battles fought in silence. Others shine with unexpected light, capturing those precious moments when healing surprised with its persistence. Like daffodils that push through frozen ground, hope has a way of finding light even in the darkest seasons.

This collection is both a reflection of personal struggle and a recognition of universal human resilience. To those walking through their own shadows: your story matters. Your pain is valid. Your healing doesn't need to follow anyone else's timeline. Some flowers bloom early, others late, but each follows its own perfect schedule.

Within these pages, you'll find both mirrors and windows— reflections of your own experiences perhaps, and glimpses into another's heart. Take what resonates, leave what doesn't. Dog-ear the pages that speak to you. Write in the margins. Let this book be a companion on your journey, whether you're in the depths of winter or witnessing your first spring blooms.

Remember, even in our darkest moments, we're not alone. Like daffodils in a field, we stand together—different heights, different stages of bloom, but all reaching toward the same light.

With hope and solidarity,

Avyneet

"Every poem here is a seed of truth, planted
in the hope that someone else's garden might grow."

TABLE OF CONTENTS
Part I: DEPRESSION

Part II: DAFFODILS

Growing Through Light

Love & Connection

Family & Roots

Wings of Freedom

PART I – DEPRESSION

THE MIRROR'S TRUTH

Leaning Against Time

Hands gripping porcelain, knuckles white,

I lean into the bathroom light.

The mirror holds a stranger's gaze—

A face transformed by harder days.

One tear breaks loose, a glacial flood,

Carving paths I never understood.

My eyes, red-stained like crushed rose petals,

Tell stories that I've left unsettled.

With trembling care,

I catch the tear,

Gentle as a makeup artist's fear

Of smudging perfect lines at dawn—

Though my perfection's long since gone.

I step away, then further still,

From this reflection, against my will.

The mirror holds someone

I should know,

But recognition's tide is low.

I cannot bear to meet those eyes

That wear my pain in stranger's guise.

This shadow-self behind the glass

Is someone

I'll pretend to pass.

In this dim bathroom's sacred space,

I've lost the map that leads to grace.

The person trapped in silver sheen

Is someone

I have never been.

Mirror Reflection - A Personal Piece

Scrubbing the bathroom tiles,
A desperate dance to silence my mind.
The spray bottle hisses,
Paper towels squeak against glass,
But I cannot meet my own gaze.
My eyes dart away from the mirror,
Like a frightened bird from thunder.
I am there, yet not there—
A ghost avoiding its own reflection,
Too afraid of the questions lurking
In those familiar eyes.
What right do I have
To face the woman in the mirror?
She holds all my broken promises,
Guards every betrayal
I've committed Against myself.
I imagine her voice breaking through:
"How could you let us fall so far?
Why did you carve these scars
Into our shared soul?
What made you turn against yourself
With such calculated precision?"
The cleaning supplies clatter in the sink
As I retreat, breath shallow,
Running from truths that echo
In this steam-clouded room.
These walls can't contain
The magnitude of my shame.

I am both prosecutor and accused,
Judge and condemned,
Standing trial before my reflection—
But I am not ready
To hear the verdict In my own eyes.

Body of Silence

My hand veins run empty now,
rivers dried of their flow.
I forget to breathe until my lungs scream,
then gasp shallow,
realizing something's been sitting
on my chest all this time.
My forehead: a war zone
where demons play tag behind sleepless eyes.
My neck stretches taut like an overtuned string,
shoulders bearing invisible mountains—
Atlas would understand this weight.
Legs have forgotten their purpose,
feet reject the earth's invitation to dance.
I lay here, chest pressed to mattress,
head propped on pillow,
face turned left like a broken compass,
thumb scrolling through endless reels
of others' darkness,
seeking mirrors of my own void.
Silent as a snowflake lost
in winter's sleeping forest,
I stare at window blinds that stare back, unsmiling.
This silence deafens—
while inside, my heart screams opera.
Fists clench then surrender,
letting everything slip through
unwilling fingers like
I'm trying to release
my own existence into the air.

A cyclone spins thoughts
into cotton candy nothing,
wants dissolving into want-nots.
Something lodges in my throat—
a bird of grief, perhaps,
or tomorrow's unspoken words—
then a deep breath held
like a secret I'll never tell.

Perfect Lives are Perfect Lies

Perfect lives are the perfect lies
Filtered through Instagram frames,
Cropped and edited till they shine
Like plastic stars in paper skies.
Behind each victory post,
A hundred battles lost to night.
Behind each perfect family photo,
Arguments swept out of sight.
They don't show the bathroom breaks
Where mascara runs in quiet streams,
Or morning coffees going cold
While anxiety steals their dreams.
Those vacation snapshots skip
The credit card debt that grows,
The fights about money and time,
The loneliness nobody knows.
Picture-perfect marriage posts
Don't capture silent dinners spent
Scrolling phones to avoid the truth
Of love that's cracked and bent.
So when they show you highlight reels,
Remember this one thing:
Perfect lives are perfect lies
We tell ourselves to feel alive.

Digital Exchange

"U okie na?"
Three words float on my screen,
Digital concern wrapped in casual text.
My fingers hover, hesitating
Over the glowing keyboard.
"Yes, just those days!
U know sometimes life happens to be life."
I type back, each word carefully chosen
To sound light, unburdened.
As if adding an exclamation mark
Could mask the weight beneath.
How strange that we've learned
To compress our darkness
Into these brief exchanges,
Where "those days" holds encyclopedias
Of unspoken struggles,
And "life happens" carries
The gravity of all our silent battles.
Behind my cheerful punctuation,
Lies a universe of unsaid things—
But maybe that's enough for now,
This gentle reaching out,
This soft acknowledgment
That someone sees through
The spaces between my words.

Guided Meditation

"Close your eyes," the instructor said, "Let's journey through your life instead." A meditation meant to heal, But memories refuse to yield.
"See yourself as newborn child, Pure joy, surrounded by smiles." But all I saw through time's dark veil: An infant, lonely, no arms to hold, No warmth to chase away the cold.
"Now five years old, with toys and play, Childhood's golden, carefree days." Yet in my mind's eye, there I sat— Silent on a lone mattress flat, A doll my only diplomat.
"Sweet sixteen, in school's embrace, Freedom written on your face." Behind closed lids, tears fought to fall, Walking empty hallway walls, No friend to answer when I'd call.
"Twenty-four, college life in bloom, Youth and friendship filling every room." But how to conjure what never was? Still standing outside joy's closed doors, Still counting scars, still keeping score.
"Thirty now, with love complete, Marriage making life so sweet." My heart just laughed a bitter sound— How craft a love I've never found? When 'enough' has stayed unbound?
"Fifty years of memories bright, Looking back at life's delight." But every year wrote pain anew, Each moment died before it flew, No golden memories shining through.

"Eighty, watching grandkids play, Satisfaction closing out your days." Yet still I saw myself alone, Scars hidden, heart turned stone, Pain the only friend I've known.

"Open eyes now, feel the peace, Let joy flow, let burden cease." But they don't understand this truth: Some souls are born to carry pain, Like trees are born to welcome rain. No meditation breaks these chains, When hurting's written in your veins.

The instructor waits for tales of light, Of burdens lifted, hearts made bright. But some wounds never find their cure, Some aches we're simply meant to endure— Born with pain, and pain ensure.

Through Glass

From my window perch,
I watch them move below—
Human rivers flowing through streets
 and sidewalks,
Flooding cafes and malls
Like they know where they're going.
But it's not their motion that haunts me.
It's their laughter,
Rising like strange music,
Their smiles breaking open
Like foreign flowers.
I press my hand against the glass,
Studying their happiness
Like a language I never learned,
An emotion coded in DNA
That somehow skipped my blood.
How do they wear joy so effortlessly?
How do their faces remember to lift at the edges?
How do their throats carry such light sounds?
I watch and wonder at this emotion—
That feels as distant as stars,
As alien as breathing underwater.
(Sometimes I think happiness
Must be a country
Where I lost my passport
long ago.)

DAILY BATTLEGROUNDS

The Fork Scrapes

Each bite is a battle,
food turned to armor,
turned to weapon,
turned to shield.
I'm shoveling it in like
I can bury something
that keeps trying to claw its way up.
My jaw works mechanically—
chew, stuff, repeat,
not even tasting,
not even swallowing.
Then suddenly—
stillness.
Food sits like clay in my mouth,
time freezes between breaths and heartbeats.
I can't lift my eyes from the plate,
can't face the world beyond this moment,
beyond this table's edge.
If atoms can split,
why can't I shrink smaller,
become invisible, fade into nothing?
The ceiling feels too high,
the room too vast.
I am terrifyingly present
in my wish to disappear.

No Excuses

I still have to do the dishes—
Watch soap bubbles rise and fall
While my thoughts sink deeper.
I still have to do the chores,
Fold laundry into neat squares
When my life feels shapeless.
I still have to make the food,
Though nothing has any taste,
Just mechanical motions of survival.
I still have to guard my tongue,
Bite back the darkness that wants to spill,
Keep being the person they expect.
I still need to change my pyjamas,
Though each button feels like lifting stone,
Each day a mountain to climb.
I still need to brush these tangles,
Make order from chaos
When my mind remains a mess.
I still have to answer every message,
Type "lol" through trembling fingers,
Force emojis through the fog.
I still have to mirror their joy,
Paint laughter on my face
When my palette's run dry.
I still need to punch the clock,
March to time's strict rhythm
When my inner music's gone silent.

I still need to make things rhyme,
Find patterns in the madness
When nothing makes sense anymore.
Because depression doesn't write
Permission slips for absence,
Doesn't excuse you from living.
Because the world keeps spinning,
Demanding its daily dues,
Even when you're barely breathing.
And they don't see the victory
In each dish washed,
Each smile forced,
Each minute survived—
They just see the person
They expect you to be.

Daily Choreography

I drink my tea and coffee cold,
sip by slow and patient sip,
drifting off on couches old,
letting mugs from fingers slip.
Stretching from my quilt cocoon to grab
what's fallen on the floor,
catching shirt-tails on door locks,
stubbing toes on bedroom doors.
Wrestling with favorite sweaters
that tangle hair and trap my head,
writing notes on palms
that wash away before the words can all be read.
Diagonal on unmade beds,
endless scrolling through the night,
eating dinner's leftover lunch,
leaving bread crusts,
marked like spite.
Pausing coffee for water's grace
when thirst demands its simple due,
knowing these aren't "normal" ways,
but they're the paths my habits drew.
Mind racing until dawn appears,
then lying dead until the noon,
when hunger's bomb or thirst's alarm
wakes me from my static moon.
Vitamins sit forgotten, waiting,
while I double-check the stove,
retrace my steps to locked doors,
seeking peace in patterns wove.

but here's what i never do:
demand others live in my kind of chaos
and here's what i must:
let souls be souls in their own wild ways
(our broken pieces don't need to match
to make something beautiful)

Hidden Struggles

When people said "Let's go to the mall,"
Only I knew about the hole in my sock,
The way my shoe's torn lining scraped my heel raw—
These secret wounds I carried,
but never talked.
When friends called "Come join us today!"
Only I knew those seven dollars meant
Either a bus ride to their laughter and play,
Or tomorrow's bread and yesterday's rent.
When they said "Let's grab a bite to eat,"
Only I knew that ten-dollar meal
 Could feed me for three days, simple but sweet—
A math equation they'd never feel.
These invitations float like autumn leaves,
Each one a reminder of what I lack.
I smile and say "Maybe next time" with ease,
While poverty whispers, holding me back.
My friends see doors wide open ahead,
While I count pennies,
unseen, unspoken—
These little "no's" pile up like bread
Crumbs marking trails of
 dreams unbroken.

Nails Turned Blue

Nails turned blue in winter's grip,
Like twilight caught beneath my skin.
Lips cracked like earth's crust in drought,
Each word a small pain seeping out.
Fingers brittle as dead leaves,
Skin paper-thin, ready to tear.
The cold seeps in through threadbare
sleeves,
While frost patterns my tangled hair.
My body maps a barren land—
Each joint a mountain, stiff with ice,
Each vein a dried-up river bed
Where warmth once flowed
at summer's price.
Mirror shows a stranger's face,
Weather-worn and winter-glazed.
These marks of cold will slowly fade,
But memory of frost stays, stays.
Like spring that waits beneath the snow,
Like seeds that dream in frozen ground,
Beneath these blues and grays,
I know
There's warmth still waiting to be found.

When Water Turns to Stone

Summer's havens mock me now—
rivers sealed in silver sleep,
lakes trapped beneath their frozen
shrouds, beaches bitter,
white and deep.
Where can a heart find shelter
when its every refuge turns to ice?
Those mountain trails that saved me
then lie buried, still as paradise.
That park bench where
I used to breathe between the world and
weighted sky stands snowbound,
offering no relief,
no place to rest or wonder why.
The sidewalk where I'd sometimes rest my
tired bones in warmer days has vanished
under winter's test,
leaving me to count the ways
that shelter slips like water through these
fingers numbed by more than cold.
When even escape routes freeze and close,
where do the weary spirits go?
Each haven locked in winter's grip leaves
me standing, lost and bare—
a bird whose branches all have shed,
whose nest has turned to frozen air.

Just In Case

i keep my phone on ring volume
at its highest peak
check it twice, three times
making sure silence hasn't crept in
while i wasn't looking
just in case (someday)
just in case (your name lights up my screen)
just in case (your voice finds its way back)
i patrol these settings
like a guard at night
protecting this possibility
this tiny hope
that refuses to die
because maybes are sweeter
than giving up
and what-ifs sing louder
than silence ever could
so i keep my phone on ring
just in case just in case
(just in case)

Silent Receipts

I read it all from preview panes—
never opening the wounds disguised as mail,
never breaking seals of envelopes that hold more
weight than paper should.
I absorb the regret they say I caused,
each failed transaction's cold report, rejections
wrapped in corporate speak:
"Unfortunately, we cannot proceed..."
I see the taunts in messages from people who once
knew my name, their silent "k" in responses like in
"known" sharp as knives, cutting shorter what was
already brief.
Some texts I leave like open graves,
no words sufficient for reply, while voicemails pile
up like autumn leaves:
"Call back, its urgent ."
and I knew urgency without making call back
The phone rings hollow to its end,
I watch it fade to missed call's mark—
can't bear to speak the truth of how my life's no
longer what they'd want to hear.
In groups, I wear my silence like a shield against
concerned hearts' probe, turn off read receipts,
stay underground, let questions echo into void.
I choose this quiet, choose this space between the
truth and what they'd hear.
(Sometimes silence is more honest than the lies we
speak to soothe.)

Remedies

That night, pain kept me company,
A tooth throbbing like a second heart—
Too fierce to ignore,
Too deep to deny.
I pressed clove oil to angry nerves,
Watched numbness spread like mercy.
Held ice against my jaw,
Until relief bloomed, brief as dawn.
But tell me—
What remedy numbs a broken heart?
What oil can sink into these deeper wounds?
What ice can freeze these memories,
That pulse like phantom teeth?
I lie awake and wonder—
Why they make medicine for every kind of pain,
Except the one that matters most.
(some aches, it seems are meant to stay awake
with us through all our darkest nights)

Unfortunately

I count applications
like sheep at night—
one, ten, hundred, thousand
clicking "submit" until
my fingers go numb
each morning brings
new emails starting with
"Unfortunately..."
until that word becomes
a knife i know by name,
"how's work?"
they ask casually
like asking about weather
and i say "good"
because how do i explain
this daily drowning?
how do i tell them
i have everything they want
on paper:
degrees like medals
experience like armor
skills sharp as swords
yet doors keep closing
in my face
like they're reading
a different resume
than the one i sent.
i've memorized
the taste of rejection

bitter as coffee gone cold
while i answer
another questionnaire
about my five-year plan
(strange how one word—
"unfortunately"—
can turn qualifications
to paper planes
flying nowhere)

Morning Weigh-In

I step on the scale each dawn
watching numbers count
not pounds but burdens
each failure drops like
lead into my bones
each regret carves away
another ounce of flesh
responsibilities weigh
heavier than gravity
disappointments subtract
from my mass daily
i am becoming less
and less and less—
measuring my disappearance
in grams,
in inches,
in square feet
of space, i dare to occupy,
shrinking smaller
until one day
i might become that speck of dust
in the corner,
too light to be touched
too small to be seen
existing
in the space between visible and gone
(how strange to feel yourself vanishing gram by gram
while still standing here)

NIGHT TERRORS

When Rooms Breathe

At night, my room becomes flesh ceiling inhales
darkness walls pulse
with forbidden rhythms
 silence grows teeth and whispers
it leans closer, closer
air turning to stone
 pressing me deeper into
a mattress that hungers
eyes bloom in shadows

multiplying like compounding equations
voices slice through dark spitting words
 i tried to outrun
i shake i sweat i hide
but phantom hands find me
corner after corner
until blankets become armor
demons paint the air black
filling empty spaces with screams
so loud , i've gone deaf to their echo
then shadow-arms wrap tight around my
breaking:
"you're safe here,
stay here everything will be alright"
(but safety tastes like suffocation when it comes
from the same darkness that's trying to devour
you)

Night Watch

I force my eyes to stay open wide,
fighting against their heavy tide.
Not tired—no,
I'm terrified that sleep
might be the longest ride.
Each yawn becomes another fight.
I pace these hours, burning bright,
because the darkness whispers lies
about the final sleep of night.
Nobody knows how much
I dread the simple act of going to bed—
how every night I shake with fear that
morning's light
 I'll never see.
So I keep watch until the dawn,
my secret guardian vigil drawn through
hours that stretch like rubber bands,
while death and sleep walk hand in hand.
I've never told a soul how
I fight sleep as if I might just die—
 how every night becomes a war
between my fears and nature's law.
My eyes burn holes into the dark.
My heart beats out its midnight mark.
I'd rather wear exhaustion's mask
than risk the sleep that might not pass.
This fear lives in me, deep and wild—
that ancient dark that swallows child
and king alike.

So here I stay,
eyes wide, until they bleed to day.
Then when sunrise paints the sky,
at last my guard can soften, die—
for daylight holds no deadly fears,
no shadows where death disappears.
In morning's safe and golden glow,
exhaustion finally lets me go.
For death, I think,
must fear the light,
and only hunts me in the night.

Dancing with Darkness

I trusted demons with my secrets ,
let shadow-hands guide me home
walked arm-in-arm with destruction
like an old friend
I became storm-chaser
dancing through cyclones
riding tsunamis
like lovers diving from cliffs
just to feel the wind
I set myself ablaze
watched skin turn to ash
scattered myself like seeds
 grew forests from my broken pieces
poison became prayer
 filling lungs with sweet decay
I murdered my ego in cold blood
hammered my smile flat
until joy forgot my address
monsters taught me new dances in rooms
where sanity fears to walk
I locked myself in iron cages
threw keys into ocean-graves
cut my wings to bone
because flying means falling
and I've tasted concrete too many times
(how strange to fear heights when you've
already hit rock bottom)

The Third Night

Three days now, and sleep's a stranger
hovering just beyond reach.
Dawn comes at 3, at 4,
whenever exhaustion finally wins its plea.
From carpet to bed and back again,
my body restless as a caged thing,
eyes fixed on shadows that dance across a ceiling
that won't stop breathing.
Left becomes right becomes left again—
a clock's hand spinning stories in dark.
My mind races through doors that should be closed,
while the night stretches endless as hunger.
The miracle is in the morning: how I rise and walk
among the living,
my face a mask of normalcy hiding nights of silent
war.
No one sees the battlefields mapped across my
sleepless mind,
how I fought through darkness only to emerge
looking fine.
These nights leave no visible scars,
no wounds that others understand— just me,
awake and wondering how long a body can command
itself to function,
move, and breathe while sleep stays locked behind
some door
where peace waits patient as a ghost on the other side
of war.

3 AM Questions

Who eats sandwiches at night?
The ones who feed their loneliness
With mayo spread too thin,
Counting crumbs in kitchen light,
While the world sleeps unaware.
Who writes poetry like fight?
Those who bleed their truth in ink,
Throwing words against the page
Like fists against their fate,
Each stanza a battle cry.
Who hides pain like a smile?
The masters of masquerade,
Painting joy in broad strokes
Over wounds still fresh—
Their lips curved in perfect lies,
While their eyes tell different stories.

HOLLOW SPACES

The Empty Room

I dream a balcony
I don't have,
where plants would grow and bloom,
where we'd sit together,
you and I, steam rising from two cups of tea.
In these dreams,
my poetry finds its perfect listener in you—
each line falling soft as leaves
between our gentle silences.
I feel your fingers in my hair,
your voice excited:
 "Let me braid!"
Your shoulder warm
against my cheek
after each sip of cooling tea.
But reality stands stark and plain:
blank walls and blinds drawn tight and low,
 a window facing empty space,
no soil, no leaves, no you at all.
Just me, alone with dreaming thoughts
 in this room that never blooms,
where plants will never drop their leaves,
where you will never braid my hair.
This space holds only shadows now,
and hopes that knock like phantom guests—
while I keep checking empty screens,
and jumping at the sounds of ghosts.

Nobody's Home

I wander through bodies
searching for doorways
that might let me in
eyes that could become windows
to rest behind hands
that might build walls around my breaking
I knock on ribcages,
hoping one might echo
with enough empty space
to fit my wandering heart
try to build homes in foreign smiles
temporary shelters in stranger's hugs
but every body is a locked house,
every touch a closed door
i became homeless
in a single night
when my heart learned it belonged nowhere
(how strange to be a ghost while still breathing)

Just Tell Me I'll Be Fine

Unstable, my hands shake
as I reach for the phone—
a lifeline to yesterday's comfort.
I call Mom, not to share victories
(there are none to speak of),
 but to hear her voice
 make the world feel less hollow.
She fills the silence
 with stories of others' success:
how someone I knew got promoted,
 how that uncle's kid made dean's list again,
 how everyone seems to be collecting gold stars
 while I'm here,
 counting carpet fibers on my bedroom floor,
salt-stained from another night
of quiet storms.
Mom, please—
 I don't need to know
who bought a house
or bought a car,
who's getting married,
who's living their dreams.
I just need you to say the words
I'm too afraid to believe myself:
 that this darkness has an end,
that I'm not lost, that I will be fine.
Don't tell me how everyone else is doing just so fine !
Just tell me I'll be fine. That's all. Just that.
Just tell me if I'll be fine ?

Will I?

Sometimes fear walks in
sits beside me for hours while I wonder—
will my lips remember how to curve upward?
will joy ever recognize my face again?
I stare at mirrors
searching for signs of life in eyes
that forgot how to shine
will I die wearing this shadow like a second skin?
is this darkness a forever-home
or just a rest stop on a longer road?
they say time heals
but what if my wounds have grown
fond of bleeding?
what if this pain has made itself
so comfortable
it's forgotten how to leave?
(sometimes i think healing isn't about going back to
who we were but learning to carry our scars with
gentler hands)

Never Served

I sat there for hours,
For days,
For weeks,
For months
For years
With empty plate
-no love was ever served to me.

Waiting

My phone stays silent
like a grave of buried hopes
no texts. no calls.
each morning i check the mailbox
as if letters could bloom there overnight
my heart dances at phantom sounds—
doorbell echoes that fade to nothing
footsteps that belong to shadows
knocks that are just the wind playing cruel games
I built a life in the space
between what is and what could be
imagining us on a balcony
that doesn't exist
drinking tea from cups
that hold only air
your fingers weaving stories
through my hair
as autumn leaves fall from plants
i never bought
but here I am in this windowless room
where dreams press against blank walls
and the only thing growing
is the darkness
between what i wish for and what i have
(how strange it is to miss someone who
never existed in a place that was never mine)

I Don't Want to Be Happy

And then came a day when I stopped chasing happiness like
it was some lost treasure I was meant to find.
"Be happy!" they say, as if joy were a switch I forgot how to
flip. Every self-help guru, every meditation guide, preaching
their gospel of gratitude like I'm some broken thing that
needs fixing.
But what if I don't want to be happy? What if I've made peace
with this quiet emptiness, this hollow space that's become
more home than happiness ever was?
I'm not dying— I'm just...here. Breathing. Existing. Is that not
enough?
Must I always be dancing? Must my lips always curve
upward? Must I collect memories like souvenirs, when my
room holds all the world I need?
They say "Travel! See the world!" But they don't understand
— every journey ends with me returning to these four walls,
to this familiar darkness that knows my name.
Why run from pain that's become a roommate? We've
learned to live together, pain and I, in this quiet agreement of
mutual existence.
Don't worry— I won't do anything drastic. I'm just learning
to exist in lower case letters, without exclamation points.
I'm fine living in grayscale when the world demands
technicolour joy.
I've found safety in this fortress of solitude, where I don't
have to pretend, where I can just...be. Isn't that also a kind of
peace?

DEPTHS AND DEMONS

Down Into the Wound

My wound isn't just deep— it's a doorway
I could step through,
a tunnel carved by years of hurt
leading down and down and down.
I walk these corridors of pain,
where walls aren't walls but memory,
red as anger, sharp as guilt, with broken glass
that catches light that isn't there.
Each step takes me deeper into darknesses I've
swallowed,
past echoes of old screams
that never found their way out.
Days blur into nights,
or maybe there was never day at all.
This place holds everything
I've lost: dreams that bled out slowly,
hope that dried up like old flowers,
promises that turned to dust.
They're all down here,
fossilized in these blood-dark halls.
I keep walking, though
I know there's no light ahead,
no warm hand reaching back,
just more tunnel, more glass, more echoes of what
broke and never healed.
Maybe I've always been here, maybe I never left—
this maze of hurt that goes so deep I could walk
forever and never find the bottom of what breaks
inside.

Why Demons

They ask why I chose demons,
As if angels were lined up,
Waiting to catch me.
When I turned around,
Searching for a hand to hold,
I found only shadows—
And shadows, at least,
Promised to stay.
So I learned to sleep
In darkness's lap,
Let demon-fingers stroke my hair,
While nightmares sang lullabies.
Because sometimes the wrong arms feel right
When they're all you've got left,
And hell's warmth burns gentler
Than heaven's cold shoulder.

(at least demons keep their promises to destroy you—
it's more than most angels ever gave)

Chemical Imbalance

I wish I could turn these poems into microscopes,
So you could see the chaos in my cells when you speak.
I wish these words were MRI machines,
Mapping the geography of hurt across my brain
Each time you turn away.
I wish I could show you the chemistry of absence—
How cortisol floods my bloodstream like a storm surge,
How dopamine starves in empty synapses,
How adrenaline screams through trembling veins.
I wish I could make poetry from proteins,
Sentences from serotonin,
Verses from racing heartbeats,
So you could read the biology of breaking.
But even science can't translate
The language of longing
Into something you would understand.

Measuring Pain

Who owns the copyright to pain? who holds the patent
on suffering?
is it in the empty echo of unanswered job applications
each rejection carving "unworthy" deeper into bone
or in the family dinner table where your victories turn
to ash in mouths that only taste what you haven't
become
maybe it lives in empty pockets that rattle with
impossible choices or in the funeral home where love
learns its final address
perhaps it's loudest in the silence of clipped wings and
buried dreams or in the note left behind by hands that
chose darkness
or does it breathe deepest in the chest of the survivor
who wakes each morning choosing life like broken
teeth
tell me— who appointed judges to measure the depth
of wounds? who created hieroglyphics to rank rivers
of tears?
pain isn't a competition ,there are no medals for
suffering ,no podium for grief to stand upon
no scorecards for trauma
your hurt doesn't need to justify its existence
doesn't need to prove its right to bleed
(pain is pain and yours is enough)

No High Places

I turn away from tower homes,
These glass-walled cages in the sky,
Where balconies hang like open palms,
And windows frame the endless why.
Even at a friend's high-rise place,
My heart beats wild against my chest.
These rooms suspended in empty space
Feel too much like an unwanted test.
Hotel windows that swing wide above
The city's distant breath—
I cannot trust what waits inside
My mind in rooms that flirt with death.
Keep me close to solid ground,
First floor, second if I must.
In heights, dark thoughts swirl round and round,
Of flying free from earthly trust.
For we are not made like the birds,
No wings to catch our desperate leap.
These thoughts I barely speak in words:
How gravity pulls thoughts too deep.
I know these walls were built to hold,
These windows made to safely frame,
But something in me, dark and old,
Whispers temptation just the same.
So ground me, root me, hold me here,
Where earth still claims me as her own.
For in these heights, I see too clear
The difference between alive and gone.

The Living Dead

There's a crack in my heart's wall
Growing wider, hungrier,
Swallowing everything inside—
A black hole made of failure.
FAILURE blazes in neon light
Across my face, my walls, my name,
Until it's all I am or see,
All I can speak or think or breathe.
Light bleeds through heart-wall fissures now,
Revealing truths I tried to flee:
Each judgment, every mocking glance,
Following street to street to street.
No new city offers refuge—
These demons know my forwarding address,
Make themselves at home in hell,
Where I've grown comfortable with flames.
Death whispers sweet escapes at night
(Coward's comfort, some might say),
But shame makes corpses of us all,
And I'm already grave-deep gone.
When laughter rings, my soul trembles
On suspension bridges frayed,
Falling through canyon depths
Where blood won't touch the ground—
I'm already ghost.
My zombies feast on what remains,
The way I gorged on dinner last,
The way I stuffed my life in bags
Before I fled my homeland's arms.

Now I sit among the shards
Of picture frames that held my dreams,
Knowing broken things stay broken,
Knowing some things can't be fixed.
Years since my lips learned to smile—
Why keep wearing this mask of flesh?
Life dealt its chances one by one,
And I collected failures like rare gems.
I died somewhere between seasons,
Summer bleeding into winter maybe,
Or winter thawing into spring—
The date's not clear, just know I'm gone.
Here lies what's left: a breathing corpse,
Still walking through the motions,
While my soul rests peaceful underground,
Buried beneath last year's snow.

3 AM Visitors

My demons come at 3 AM, pull up chairs
make themselves at home
in the hollow of my chest
they wear familiar faces
speak in voices, i've known since childhood
call me by my secret names
"remember when," they whisper
opening old wounds
like photo albums "remember how you failed?"
they show me others' victories
not to spark envy, but to carve deeper
the shape of my shortcomings
"see how far they've climbed?"
they say, while measuring
the distance between, my dreams and reality
"see how small you are?"
they whisper, comparing
my struggles to others' effortless flight
we sit together, in darkness thick as tar
while they list my fears, like grocery items
they know exactly where
to press their fingers
which scars to reopen, which doubts to water
sometimes i wonder, if they live inside me
or if i live inside them, our borders blurred by time
we've grown so used, to each other now—
these midnight visitors, these shadow companions
(perhaps the scariest thing about demons
is not their cruelty but how familiar
their voices become in the dark)

WEIGHT OF LIVING

Catalogue of Fears

I'm afraid of heights that hunger,
Of needles seeking softest sight,
Of unknown eyes that pierce like bullets
Through the armor of my night.
When earthquakes shake the steady ground,
No shelter waits with open arms—
Just earth's crust splitting wide its jaw
To swallow me in molten harm.
I see the circle closing in,
Their laughter sharp as broken glass,
While bottles rain and stones take flight,
And still they smile as I pass.
I dream of being lost in nowhere,
No voice to call, no hand to hold,
Just endless paths that lead to paths
In landscapes neither new nor old.
I see myself in winter woods,
Leg bleeding trails through virgin snow,
While wolves close in from darkness deep
And snowflakes build my tomb below.
But deeper than these mortal fears,
More primal than the fear of pain,
I'm terrified of death's swift hand
Before I've learned to live again.
This is the fear that haunts me most:
Not that my heart will cease to beat,
But that it never truly lived—
That death will find me incomplete.

A Place to Rest

I dream of walls that know my name,
A door that opens to only my key,
A space that holds me
Without charging rent for breathing.
Somewhere to return to when battles
Leave me bloodied,
Where I can lay down my armor
Without worrying about next month's war.
A shelter where silence doesn't cost,
Where darkness doesn't send bills,
Where I can hibernate with my wounds
Until they remember how to heal.
No one counting my tears,
No borrowed corners in others' lives—
Just my own four walls
That won't ask me to explain
Why I need to disappear.
Because sometimes warriors
Need to retreat from the world,
Curl up in their own fortress
Until their strength returns.
I dream of a home
That won't evict me for failing,
That won't demand victory as payment,
That will simply let me be
Until I'm ready to fight again.
(Because even soldiers need a place
To lay down their shields
And remember how to breathe.)

They Waited

They sat at the edge of my darkness,
Feet dangling over despair,
Telling me how patient they were being.
"We're right here,"
They called down into my drowning.
"We haven't left,"
As if presence was the same as rescue.
They made waiting sound like heroism,
Turned their inaction into virtue,
While water rose around my neck.
"Isn't it enough?"
They asked from their safe perch
Above my dying.
"That we stayed to watch?"
But what good are witnesses
Who won't throw rope?
What use are hands
That only wave as you go under?
They stayed until the end,
Proud of their loyalty to my grave.
(They say they never left,
But sometimes staying still
Is just another way of walking away.)

Fragile Contents

I marked it clearly:
HANDLE WITH CARE
FRAGILE DREAMS INSIDE
THIS WAY UP
placed my innocence
in bubble wrap
lined the box
with tender hopes
but they tossed it
in with all the rest
just another package
on the truck of life
bouncing through potholes
tumbling off shelves
while i watched
the tracking updates
helplessly
when it came back
"return to sender—
refused without reason"
I opened the box
with trembling hands
found my dreams
in pieces
white china shattered
to stardust
they say you can fix
broken things with gold
make them beautiful
in their breaking

but what about
the fragments too small
to gather?
the dust of innocence
that slipped through fingers
scattered in wind?
(some things
once shattered
can't be glued back
whole—
they become part
of the air we breathe
invisible reminders
of what we lost)

Uncertainty

I work until my fingers forget
they're fingers
until my eyes burn
with screen-light dreams
then body rebels
demands its moment
of horizontal truth
on unmade beds
and there they come—
those spinning thoughts
those midnight whispers:
"will any of this matter?"
uncertainty crawls in
through tired windows
sits heavy on my chest
asks questions i can't answer
but here's the truth
i've learned to tell myself:
the future never shows
its cards in advance
you can't know the ending
until you write it
can't see the view
until you climb
victory and failure
are patient guests—
they'll wait their turn
to show their faces

but first
these hands must finish
what they started
these dreams must find
their final form
(sometimes courage
is just continuing
when uncertainty
pulls up a chair
and tries to make
itself at home)

Fear of Change

I get mean when I hear
about home changing
without my permission
my heart turns bitter
at news of progress:
that kid in high school now
that friend with a new job
that wild soul grown sensible
that dirt road finally paved
it's not that I don't want
good things for them
it's just—
every change feels like
a clock ticking louder
a reminder of how long
I've been away
fear sits beside me
applauding each update
whispering:
"hurry, hurry
or you'll miss it all"
I'm afraid one day
I'll return to find
my memories homeless
the places where i lost myself
rewritten in concrete
and chrome
afraid the corners
where i hid my youth

will be renovated
beyond recognition
what if I can't find
the pieces of me
I left scattered
in those familiar spaces?
what if home
moves on without me
and I return
a stranger to my own story?
(sometimes the hardest part
of being away
is knowing that places
don't pause
just because we're not there
to watch them change)

Money Before Philosophy

They only listen to wisdom
wrapped in success stories
pearls of truth
must come with price tags
philosophy sounds sweeter
from penthouse views
words carry more weight
when spoken from heights
no one follows footprints
of those still climbing
they wait to hear life lessons
from those who've reached the peak
empty pockets make
empty speeches
no matter how pure
the truth they hold
the world bows deeper
to golden thoughts
than copper wisdom
worn thin by struggle
(strange how truth
needs currency
to prove its worth—
how wisdom must
wear wealth
to be heard)

Curated Truth

They want me to speak
in highlight reels—
only victories, only trophies, only light
"tell us about your wins," they say
"your medals, your mountains climbed
your battles won"
as if life is a museum
where we display
only masterpieces
hiding the sketches
that bled through paper
they call it optimism
this careful curation
of joy without shadows
success without struggle
strength without breaking
but isn't half-truth
just lying softly?
isn't silence about darkness
another kind of dark?
how can anyone see
the whole of me through this
cleaned-up gallery
of perfect moments?
(sometimes the most honest thing
about victory
is the story of how many times
we lost before we won)

Solo Home

I've forgotten the sound
of doorbells ringing
the rhythm of footsteps
approaching my door ,now I'm both
the leaving and returning
the one who turns on lights
in empty rooms
after work, I rest
on the quiet couch
but must rise again
my own caretaker
for water, for food
for all the small things
that used to be shared
so l find excuses
to stay in lit places—
lingering in restaurants
where voices fill the air
walking slower on streets
where people still exist
trying to stretch
these moments of light
before returning
to rooms where silence has made itself
too much at home
(sometimes loneliness
isn't in the being alone but in forgetting
what it felt like not to be)

PART II - DAFFODILS

SEEDS OF HEALING

The Path Back

I am grateful for each failure
that brought me to my knees
because there—
on the ground of my breaking
I found footprints
leading backward,
grateful for every closed door
that forced me to sit
in my own silence
until i heard
that small voice crying
from years ago,
thankful for the walls
I kept hitting, until my adult armor cracked
revealing the child within
still holding
all those unspoken hurts,
who knew it would take falling apart
to find the pieces, I left behind?
who knew
growing up
meant growing backward
to heal forward?
(sometimes our failures
are just detours
leading us back
to the healing
we've been running from)

For the first time

For the first time,
I laid my shield to rest.
Let the cut breathe open,
Watched crimson rivers flow.
The arrow stayed lodged,
A memorial to pain.
I sat with my wounds,
Not to heal, but to feel—
To know I could still sense
Something, anything at all.
These precious seconds of being alive
Before the darkness falls.

The Strength to Stay

Even after everything, I tell myself I'm strong enough
— strong enough to stay breathing, to keep my feet
planted on this tired earth.
But in the quiet hours, when truth slips through the
cracks of certainty, I wonder: Is this strength coursing
through my veins, or just the hollow echo of not being
brave enough to leave?
What do you call this force that keeps me here?
Courage wearing survival's mask? Or fear dressed up
as strength— afraid of both the darkness and the light?
Maybe it's neither. Maybe it's both. Maybe strength
lives in this very questioning, in these hands that
shake but still reach for tomorrow, in this heart that
breaks but won't stop beating.
Perhaps true courage hides in the simple act of asking
why we stay, while staying all the same.

All of Us, Human

I let them go at last—these grudges I carried like
stones in my pockets,
watched them evaporate like morning fog until
nothing remained but clear sky.
I made peace with imperfections, mine and theirs, all
our jagged edges that never quite fit together right.
My shoulders ached from carrying
so much for so long—bags packed with heavy
histories, while I screamed into deaf winds, lungs
burning: "Look at these wounds! See this pain!"
But they walked past like zombies, already dead to
feeling, and I couldn't understand how they felt
nothing when I felt everything.
I'd locked my trauma in a box, stored it safe inside my
blood pumping device with a deep closet, built cages
in my joints to hold each memory that hurt.
Then one by one, I opened them— every lock, every
door, every cage.
Let each captured bird take wing,
watched them scatter to open sky.
I left my wounds uncovered,
let them breathe in open air,
finally understanding:
we're all just humans trying to heal.
Some days we're falling apart, some days we're
somehow doing just fine. Some days we're just
breathing ,filling empty spaces in throat and lungs.

One Wound at a Time

You're right—
these wounds aren't butterflies
that flutter away
when we open our hands,
each cut needs its own time,
its own medicine,
its own quiet attention,
some need years
of gentle cleaning,
daily bandage changes,
careful watching,
others need decades
of patient tending
before they learn to close,
we can't rush healing
like we can't rush dawn
some scars need to be
looked at every morning
until they fade
into softer stories,
this is the slow work
of becoming whole—
not letting go
but letting heal
one wound at a time
until the bandages aren't needed anymore.
(healing isn't about forgetting the wounds
but about not having to check them every hour
to see if they're still bleeding)

Pain Seeks Attention

Pain is a child
tugging at your sleeve,
throwing tantrums in your chest,
screaming in your bones,
the more you turn away,
pretending not to hear
the louder it becomes—
breaking dishes in your ribs,
drawing on your lungs
with permanent markers,
pulling fire alarms
in your nervous system,
it doesn't want much,
this orphaned feeling
just someone to kneel down
look it in the eyes
and say:
"i see you
i hear you
i'm here"
but we keep walking faster
covering our ears
until pain learns
to speak in fever,
to write in bruises,
to paint in sleepless nights,
all it ever wanted
was to be held

like any child
crying out
in the dark
(sometimes healing starts
not with medicine
but with the simple act
of turning around
and finally
listening)

Still Remember

I remember everything—
precise as crime scene photos
temperature of the air
angle of the sun
color of the walls
time frozen on clocks
these moments that stole pieces of me:
the first time i learned
I wasn't enough
the day fairy tales
turned to dust
each memory carved
with surgeon's precision:
the exact shade of shame
the weight of self-doubt
the texture of trust
breaking like thin ice
i've changed everything since—
new friends, new places
new skin, new face
but these memories
still know my address
I want to mail them back
return to sender
mark them "no longer
at this address"
but they keep finding me
like letters with wings

I am not that person anymore
but that person's pain
still lives in my bones
like hidden splinters
that surface in rain.
(how strange that time
can change everything
except the sharpness
of certain memories
that refuse to blur)

The Courage to Begin

I gather all my broken pieces
like seeds in trembling hands
ready to plant them
in fresh soil,
it takes such bravery
to believe in growing
after being shattered
after being scattered,
to trust that roots
can find their way
through rubble,
toward light to have faith
that winter-worn hearts
can learn to bloom in spring soil,
such courage it takes
to start again,
when memory knows
the cost of failing,
yet here i stand
with hope-filled palms
ready to plant
these pieces of me,
watching how pain
transforms to petals,
how endings become
beginnings.
(sometimes bravery is just the quiet act
of planting yourself one more time)

FINDING PEACE

Settling Waters

Eventually all waves settle,
no matter how high they rose
how fierce they crashed
how wild they danced,
the angriest storms
find their quiet,
the roughest seas
learn to whisper,
even tsunami hearts
return to stillness
after they've spent
their fury,
nature knows
this simple truth:
nothing stays turbulent
forever,
the ocean always
remembers how
to smooth its face
like glass.
(perhaps peace
isn't something
we chase
but something
we return to
like waves
coming home
to calm)

I Know Me

I've lived in this skin
since first breath
walked every step
of this journey
I was there
for every tear shed
every laugh that broke free
every dawn that cracked open
I watched myself
grow through seasons
bloom and wither
rise and fall
I know the map
of my own heart
every scar's story
every dream's birthplace
yet strangers walk in
with borrowed wisdom
telling me who I am
like they've lived
my lifetime in a day
they point at parts of me
label them "broken"
find flaws in places
I never knew were wounds,
they speak of my shadows
as if they held the light,
diagnose insecurities
I never carried

but how can they know
the geography of my soul
when they've never walked
these inner landscapes?
(i am my own
longest conversation—
no tourist guide
can tell me
about the country
I've always lived in)

I Choose Grace

They turned their fingers
into arrows
aimed at all my
supposed flaws,
their laughter followed me
like shadows,
their smirks hung
in air like smoke
"imperfect," they said
"impractical," they laughed
as if they were made
of polished marble
and oh, how many times
I could have turned
their own mirrors
back at them,
could have listed
their every crack
counted their own
imperfections
but i kept my fingers
folded in peace
kept my observations
tucked away
because i refuse
to join their circus
of pointing fingers
and cruel laughter

i'd rather be
the target of arrows
than become another
archer of pain
and never become
what I don't like
(sometimes strength
isn't in what you do
but in what you
choose not to do)

Nothing to Hold

Even breath is borrowed—
inhaled for a moment
then released back
to the waiting world
we own nothing
not even the tears
that slip through fingers
back to earth
so why do we clutch
at passing moments?
why cage butterflies
of fleeting joy?
let everything flow
like wind through trees
like rivers to seas
like stars through night,
even love
needs freedom
to dance its own way
through open skies
(perhaps peace lies
in understanding
we're just temporary
keepers of gifts
meant to keep
moving)

The Braid

She holds her story
in strands of hair—
each length a chapter
of survival,
when life tangles
into chaos,
she sits before
her mirror-confidant
patient fingers
sorting through knots
like untangling
memories
smoothing rough edges
of yesterday's storms
three sections:
past, present, future
weaving together
in practiced rhythm,
each crossing
a small victory each twist
a letting go until finally
the rubber band snaps
into place holding together
all she's overcome ready now
to begin again her strength bound
in this simple ritual of remaking
(some women carry their courage in braided rope
down their backs— a spine made of stories)

Between Thoughts

In the pause
between one thought
and the next
in that brief infinity
where mind holds its breath
before spinning again
there lies a space
vast as oceans
quiet as moonlight,
where worries haven't learned
how to swim,
where fears forget
their own names,
a moment suspended
like dew before falling
like birds between wingbeats
like stars between blinks,
here, in this gap
this holy silence
this precious nothing,
peace spreads its wings
if only for a heartbeat
before thoughts return
like eager children
(sometimes serenity
lives not in the thinking
but in the spaces
where thoughts
forget to be)

GROWING THROUGH LIGHT

Acceptance

Life never offered me a menu
never asked my preferences
about pain or peace
it served what it had—
bitter herbs and broken bread
storms without shelter
paths without bridges
no chance to say
"i'd rather not"
no space to whisper
"maybe something else"
so I learned to swallow
whatever filled my plate
learned to call survival
by another name:
acceptance
(sometimes the only choice
we get
is how we carry
what we never chose)

Meeting Him Again

All these years i carried him—
this child who had everything
except what his eyes searched for
loved, but not in the language
his heart could understand
I ignored his quiet knocking
rushed past his closed door
became another adult
too busy for his stories
too grown for his tears
until one day
pain brought me to my knees
and there he was
sitting cross-armed on the pavement
anger carved in small lips
sadness pooled in silent eyes
I wanted to reach out
gather all his hurt
into my adult arms
but we were strangers now
separated by years
of looking away,
he sits there still
in his fortress of silence
while i learn slowly
how to become
the friend he never had,
maybe one day

we'll build bridges
across these years
heal wounds that echo
through time
maybe then
we can both learn
how to play again
(it's strange—
becoming the adult
you needed
when you were small
and finding the child
still waiting
for someone
to understand)

Things I Never Had

I wish for memories I never made—
Someone's warm hand against my back
As I climb school steps,
Someone's ears waiting
To catch stories of my day.
I dream of little fingers
Wrapped in bigger ones,
Dancing down sidewalks
To stores that hold promises
Of unexpected toys,
Given for no reason
Except love.
I wish I could've been
The stubborn child
Crying rivers for candy
Instead of this adult
Who learned too young
That tears change nothing.
I never wanted this armor
Called strength—
It came uninvited,
Murdered the child inside,
Left this hollow adult
Who carries grocery bags
Alone.
My soul stands confused
At the crossroads
Of need and survival,
Wanting to reach out

But keeping eyes down,
As if the ground
Holds safer secrets.
I've learned to walk
These streets alone,
No shield but silence,
No shelter but locked doors,
While something inside
Still whispers:
"I wish..."
(They say growing up
Means leaving childhood behind,
But no one talks about
The children who never got
To be children at all.)

Words That Stay

I wish I could unhear
those first cruel words
that taught me
childhood had borders
they arrived without warning—
from adult lips
or children's mouths
equally sharp
equally permanent
now years have passed
decades have turned
but those words still echo
louder than church bells
clearer than morning,
I want to find you
after all this time
tell you how your syllables
became stones I carried
in my pocket for years
how they took something
I didn't know
could be taken
until it was gone
now as I heal
stitch by careful stitch
I see this trail behind me—
words strung together
like heavy beads
dragging like a wedding train
of collected hurts

I'm ready to cut
this thread of memory
let those words fall
like autumn leaves
scatter in wind
because I want to dance
at my own wedding
to joy
without the weight
of your voice
pulling me back
(sometimes healing
means learning
to unhear
what we can't
forget)

The Final Step

After healing each version of me—
the wounded child
the guarded teenager
the broken adult
after bandaging every memory
cleaning each infected regret
learning to hold trauma
with gentler hands
I want to gather them all—
every person who knew me when
I was drowning in my pain
call them to witness
this transformation
I want to hear them say
"you're different now
you've bloomed
while we weren't looking"
but here's the truth
I'm still learning:
this need for their eyes
to validate my healing
is just another child
waiting at the window
for someone to notice
I'm still working
on this last wound—
this hunger
to prove to everyone

that those broken pieces
weren't really me
just the weight
I carried
(perhaps the final step
of healing
is learning that
the only validation
that matters
is the quiet pride
of your own heart
recognizing itself
in the mirror)

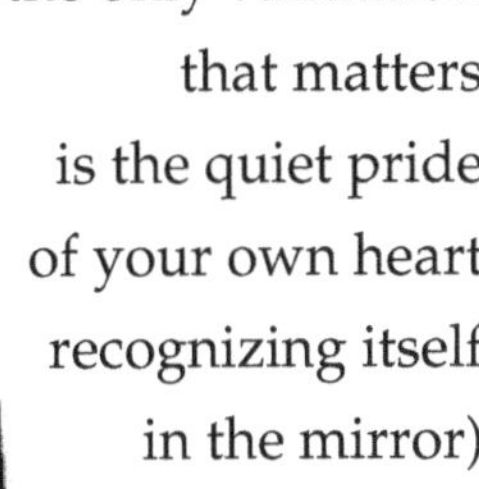

Like Butterflies in Rain

Today I learned that butterflies
know when to fold their wings
and wait for storms to pass
they don't fight the rain
that could tear their colors
don't blame themselves
for needing shelter,
they rest,
knowing pause
isn't permanent
knowing flight
will return
so maybe it's okay
to fold ourselves small
when life pours too heavy
to step back from the storm
that threatens to break us
let them think
you've forgotten how to fly
let them mistake
your rest for retreat
you know the truth:
that even dormant seeds
hold gardens in their hearts
that rainbows only come
after clouds have spent
themselves empty
this pause is not your end

it's just your wings
gathering strength
for the moment
when skies clear
(sometimes the bravest thing
isn't flying through storms
but knowing when
to wait them out)

The Morning I Chose Myself

Between cold coffee and client calls,
I've been holding my breath for years.
Playing dress-up in a responsible adult's life,
Excel sheets where poems used to be.
Remember that girl who wrote stories
under blankets with a flashlight?
She's still here, hiding between
calendar blocks and email chains,
smuggling dreams into lunch breaks.
My screen shows another deadline,
Another meeting in ten minutes,
Another day of being the reliable one.
But something cracks this morning—
quiet as milk dripping from a spoon,
loud as a heart finally choosing truth.
They say I'm having a quarter-life crisis,
call me crazy for considering freedom
over a perfectly stable prison.
"Think about your visa," they warn,
"Your savings, your future security."
As if security ever fed a hungry soul.
At mid twenties, you're supposed to build
foundations, not burn them to ash.
But what if these walls I've built
are just pretty cages, painted
in professional shades of success?
Through my window, autumn leaves dance,
free and wild—everything I'm not.

A bird lands on my cramped balcony,
stares at me in my wrinkled pajamas,
my coffee growing colder with each
unfinished calculation.
Yes, I'm terrified. Yes, my hands shake
when I think about tomorrow.
But being terrified and being sure
can live in the same heart—
mine is one of those.
Better an empty bank account than an empty life.
Better to leap now than spend forever wondering
what lies beyond these perfectly formatted cells.
Some dreams cost everything
because they're worth everything.
And maybe that's the point—
maybe the scariest choices
are the only ones worth making.
So here I am, another morning
of pretending to be practical,
watching my reflection fade
in a laptop screen gone dark.
But today feels different.
Today, I choose the girl
who still believes in magic,
who writes poems between
client calls, who refuses
to die by spreadsheet.
They say smart people look before they leap.
But sometimes the smartest thing
is to trust you'll learn
to fly on the way down.

Becoming Light

I learned to make my own light
when darkness stayed too long
started small— just a spark
in my chest where hope lives
learned to fan that tiny flame
with gentle breath and patient hands
now i carry my own sun
beneath my ribs between heartbeats
no more waiting for external stars
to guide me home
through shadowed paths
I've become my own dawn
 my own torch
my own northern light
glowing from inside
 like bioluminescent seas
creating magic from my depths
(sometimes the brightest light
 isn't what we seek
but what we learn to become)

LOVE & CONNECTION

Clean love

To love you
I cleanse my hands
like preparing
for prayer
wash away the world
sanitize doubt
dry each finger
until they shine
only then
do I dare touch
this love we share—
pure as new-fallen snow
gentle as white cashmere
against winter skin
precious as silk
passed down through generations
I handle your heart
like the finest shawl
woven from clouds
and morning light
(some loves
require such careful
handling—
as if touching
something holy)

Two Healing Hearts

We were just children really—
wearing adult skin
like borrowed clothes
when we found each other
young and stumbling
through career paths
and growing pains
connected across miles
by invisible strings
we made mistakes
beautiful and terrible
learning life's grammar
through trial and error
sitting cross-legged
on bedroom floors
unwrapping years
of hidden hurts
you with antiseptic
me with bandages
teaching each other
the gentle art
of healing
we fought like planets
breaking orbit
screamed and cried
and tried to run
but that rubber band
of understanding
always pulled us
back to center

two wounded souls
learning to clean
each other's scars
figuring out life
one bandage at a time
what mattered wasn't
our perfect moments
but how we stayed
through all the mess
of becoming whole
(sometimes love
is just two broken people
holding space
while each other
learns to heal)

A Different Kind of Perfect

I no longer dream
of candlelit promises
or diamond-studded forevers
instead, I wish for something
more precious:
two souls who understand
healing has its own clock
I want gentle hands
that know how to hold
both strength and softness
words that remember
their own weight
before they fall
not the perfect family
from television screens
but two people who know
how broken pieces
fit together
who understand
that love isn't about
never fighting
but about fighting fair
keeping voices low
when little ears listen,
I dream of building
a home where trauma
doesn't pass down
like inherited china

where children never learn
to tiptoe around anger
or translate silence
into blame
where "i'm sorry"
isn't a stranger
and "i love you"
isn't saved
for special occasions
where our children whisper
"my parents are like
Romeo and Juliet"
but with a happier ending—
a love so pure it makes
fairy tales seem pale
this is my new romance:
not roses and rings
but the quiet art
of growing whole
together
(because sometimes
perfect isn't about
never breaking
but about knowing
how to heal
as one)

Simple Answers

"i have no car"
"i'll walk"
"i'm not so good"
"i love you"
"i overthink a lot"
"i'll explain everything"
"my stories are long"
"i have time"
"i can do it myself"
"i know you can, but let me"
"i have nothing"
"let me stay by your side"
"i don't know how to do it"
"we'll figure it out together"
(sometimes love
is just the perfect reply
to all our
imperfect confessions—
turning 'i' into 'we')

Evidence of Love

I am my own proof
that love exists—
not in theory
not in stories
but in flesh and bone
I carry it
like oceans carry salt
like stars carry light
like earth carries spring
it fills me
to overflowing
spills from my edges
like sunshine through leaves
i don't need
external evidence
when I am living proof
of love's existence
my heart beats
its own testimony
my breath writes
love's biography
(what better proof
of love's reality
than a soul
saturated with it?)

Not Ready to Let Go

They speak of leaving
like it's simple math—
pros lined up against cons
neat columns of reason
they offer metaphors
of ill-fitting shoes
and practical paths
while I bite my tongue
because how do I tell them
that love isn't solved
like equations?
that hearts don't follow
logic's clean lines?
they ask for validation
of their letting go
while I wonder—
couldn't we hold on
just a little longer?
squeeze a little tighter?
try one more time?
when they compare love
to shoes that don't fit
I want to say:
sometimes it's just
the socks that need changing
sometimes a bit of cotton
fills the empty spaces
sometimes we adjust
the laces differently

they call me impractical
this heart that would rather
bear the blisters
than donate its favorite shoes
to stranger's feet
this blessing and curse—
this stubborn belief
that love deserves
every chance
every adjustment
every attempt at repair
(maybe I'm wrong
to keep wearing
what others would discard
but some of us were built
to bear the rubbing
of imperfect fits
if it means keeping
what we love)

He Had Time

Every time I warned
"it's a long story"
bracing for the usual
polite escape
he simply smiled and said
"I have time"
like he was offering
the rarest gift 
no rushing rivers
of conversation
no glancing at phones
or watching doors
just the gentle art
of being present
of making space
for untold chapters
he gave my words
room to breathe
let my stories
unfold like flowers
opening at their own pace
(sometimes love
is just someone
who makes time
stretch like summer
evenings
when you need
to be heard)

Best of All

I used to trace old scars
from hearts that didn't
know how to love me right
counted tears shed
over people who treated
love like a game
but then you walked in—
like the universe saying
"oh, you thought that was love?
wait till you see this"
now I understand
why everyone else
let me go—
they were making space
for something
cosmic
(sometimes hearts break
in all the right places
to let in
the light)

Wrong Turns Right

I'm thankful for every wrong turn—
those midnight detours
those stumbled steps
those paths I wasn't meant to take
grateful for all my errors
like breadcrumbs leading
to where you waited
without knowing you waited
each mistake was just
another step in the dance
that brought me here
to this exact moment
who knew getting lost
could be so precise?
that wrong turns
could map the right way?
now I understand
why my compass spun wild
why my stars misaligned
why my roads all twisted
they were just
choreographing
the perfect way
to find you
(sometimes the best destinations
are the ones we reach
by accident)

He Drew Flowers

I tried to hide
my past's sharp lines
pulling sleeves
over wrist-written stories
but he took my hand
so gently that fear
forgot how to breathe
as he pushed back fabric
I squeezed my eyes shut
heart stumbling
over its own beat
expecting judgment
finding art instead—
his fingers turning
old wounds into gardens
drawing delicate petals
around each scar
making flowers bloom
where pain once grew
he didn't try to erase
what was written there
just added beauty
to the margins
(sometimes love
doesn't heal by hiding
but by making art
from our broken places)

To Be Closer

I wish I could build bridges
from heartbeat to heartbeat
spanning oceans
connecting continents
imagine sliding down
rainbow roads
that make borders
blur like watercolors
I'd pull land masses
close as puzzle pieces
until they click
into single soil
maybe I could empty
oceans with a straw
sip by patient sip
until seafloors become 
highways for walking feet
turn waters into windows
turn distances to doorways
make far places
next-door neighbors
just so I could be
close enough
to hear your laugh
without time zones
getting in the way
(some hearts are too connected
to understand why maps drew them so far apart)

Love's Truth

When life crashes in
with all its weight
you learn some truths:
that love isn't always
the heaviest burden
when bills pile up
like autumn leaves
when health slips
through trembling fingers
when dreams collapse
like paper houses
and yet—
love remains
the deepest wound
the sharpest blade
the softest bruise
how strange, that it can be
both everything
and nothing, all at once
the smallest worry
in a storm of concerns
yet still the ache
that keeps you awake
when larger pains
have gone to sleep
(perhaps this is why poets never tire
of writing about love— it's both the wound
and the bandage, the poison and the cure)

Standing Tall

I loved myself today—
stood up straight
spoke my truth
let boundaries bloom
and suddenly gravity shifted
weights i didn't know
I carried fell from my shoulders
like autumn leaves
I grew taller with each "no"
stronger with each "not anymore"
felt my soul stretch its wings
shake off years of others' expectations
such lightness comes
from loving yourself enough
to draw lines in permanent ink
no more piggyback rides
for others' dreams
no more shrinking to fit their frames
i choose now to love my edges
my shadows my wild dreams
to protect my peace
like the precious garden
it has always been
(sometimes freedom is just learning to love yourself
louder than any voice that says you shouldn't)

FAMILY & ROOTS

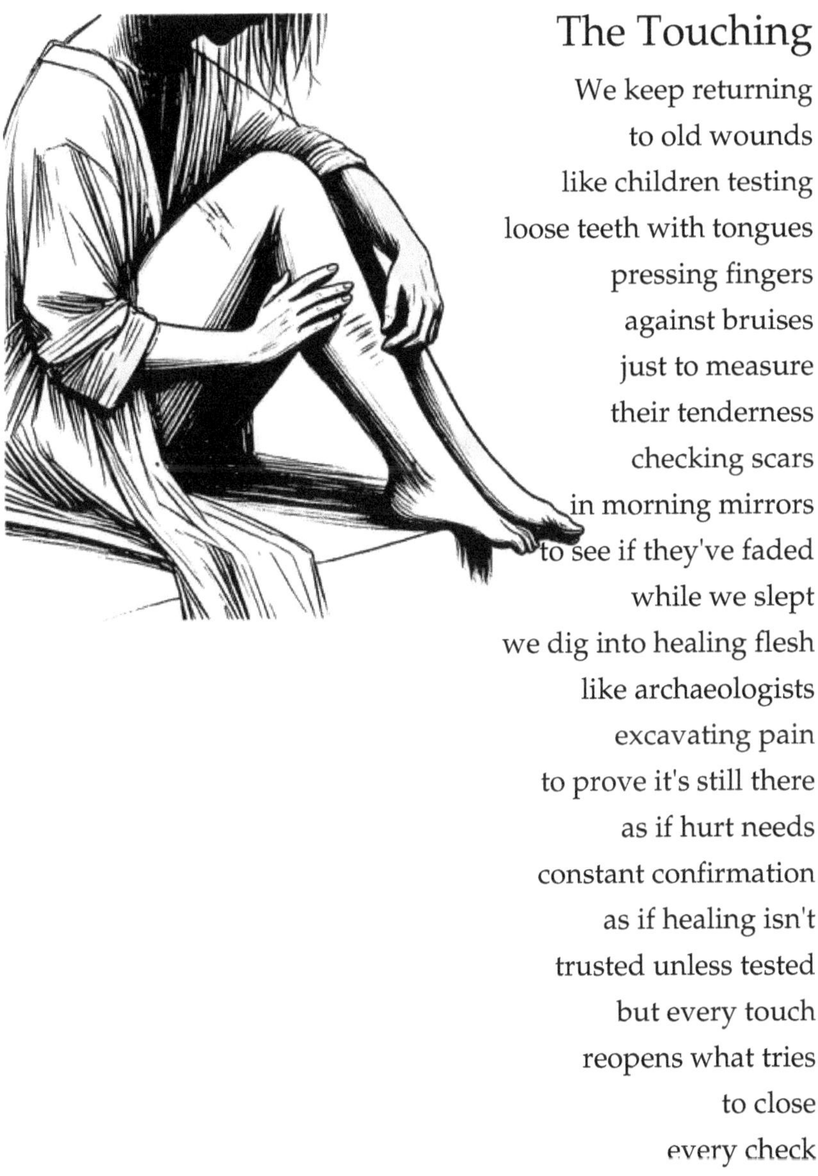

The Touching

We keep returning
to old wounds
like children testing
loose teeth with tongues
pressing fingers
against bruises
just to measure
their tenderness
checking scars
in morning mirrors
to see if they've faded
while we slept
we dig into healing flesh
like archaeologists
excavating pain
to prove it's still there
as if hurt needs
constant confirmation
as if healing isn't
trusted unless tested
but every touch
reopens what tries
to close
every check
keeps the wound
fresh and weeping
(maybe healing starts with learning to keep our
hands by our sides letting scabs form undisturbed)

What Adults Decide

I sit among them—
these adults deciding
fates like they're choosing
dinner menus
they speak of divorce
like weather patterns,
of separation
like business deals,
of children's futures
like they're moving chess pieces
I stay quiet
knowing my thoughts
would sound too much
like fairy tales
in this room of
practical decisions,
if I could rewrite
this child's story
I'd ink it with wonder—
stuff their days
with teddy bears
that never lose their hugs
parents who never
lose their way back home
love that never learns
how to break
no therapist couches
waiting in their future
no journals filled

with questions about why,
no wounds to check
like weather forecasts
but here I sit
watching adults
carve up childhood
with practical knives
while i hold these wishes
like forbidden stories
in my throat
if only life
could be written
in crayon dreams
instead of legal ink
if only we could protect
their once-upon-a-times
from our ever-afters
(sometimes the most
painful part
of growing up
is watching others
lose their chance
at fairy tales)

Broken families are broken crayons

They tell me
"broken crayons still color"
as if that makes up
for the snap
the crack
the pieces that don't fit
right anymore,
imagine being a child
opening a Christmas gift-wrapped box
heart full of rainbow dreams
fingers trembling with hope
only to find
all your colors
already broken
how dare they tell
this disappointed heart
"but look—
it still makes flowers
still draws suns
still works just fine"
as if function
could replace
the joy of wholeness
as if "still works"
could heal
the first sharp sting
of broken things

yes, broken homes
can still shelter,
broken families
can still love,
broken crayons
can still color
but don't tell me
the breaking
doesn't matter,
don't tell a child
clutching pieces
of what should be whole,
that broken
is just as good
as never broken
at all
(some truths
are too heavy
for children's hands—
like learning early
that sometimes life
gives us broken things
and expects us
to color anyway)

Growing Up Too Fast

I think about this child
who still believes
in whole things
sleeping in dinosaur sheets
while his world splits
like continents drifting
he doesn't know yet
that mama's turned back
and dada's couch nights
are rehearsals for goodbye
doesn't understand
this family trip
is the final page
of a closing book
his small hands
still reach for both
not knowing they'll soon
stretch across planets
that never align
how will he learn
that school pickup
won't be a two-seat story
anymore?
his world will tear
like construction paper
edges rough and ragged
forcing him to live
in pieces

mama counting pennies
for grocery lists
dada missing parent-teacher
meetings again
this tiny astronaut
with cartoon-character smile
space-ship lunch box
rocket-ship dreams
must now grow tall enough
to bridge galaxies
his child-bones
forced to stretch
beyond their years
(how heavy the universe
becomes
when it lands
on shoulders
still learning
to carry their own
weight)

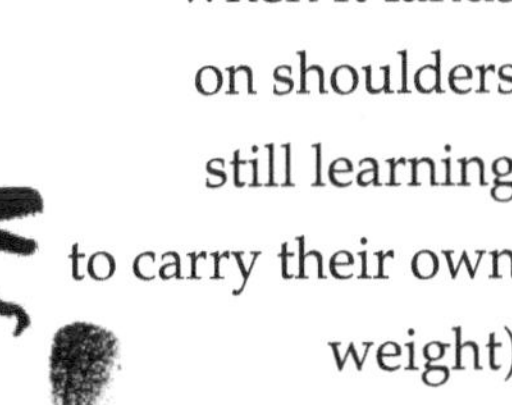

To My Seventeen-Year-Old Self

One random evening
between thoughts
I saw her—
my seventeen-year-old self
still carrying burdens
I forced her to bear
I'm sorry, sweet girl
for making you
everyone's shelter
when you needed
shelter yourself
I'm sorry for teaching you
that love must be earned
through sacrifice
that "good girls" swallow
their own needs
like bitter medicine
I watched you forget
how to smile
your face settling
into neutral masks
your laughter buried
under others' expectations
I made you believe
your worth lived
in others' approval
taught you to shrink
to fit their comfort
but now I see

what I did to you—
how I let them
carve pieces from you
until you forgot
your own shape
today i set you free
from all these chains
I wrapped around you
let you breathe
without permission
laugh without reason
sweet seventeen
it wasn't your job
to be everyone's savior
to make yourself smaller
so others could feel big
(I'm learning now
how to mother
the girl I once was
how to love her
back to life)

Missing Me

I have nostalgia
not for places
but for a version of myself
I left behind somewhere
I miss her—
that girl who knew how
to laugh without checking
if joy was appropriate
who danced through rooms
like gravity was optional
who moved to rhythms
only her heart could hear
who didn't calculate
the cost of broken things
or measure months
in due dates and rent checks
who climbed stairs
like they were mountains
to conquer
each step its own adventure
whose dreams weren't yet
weighted down by practicality
whose smile hadn't learned
to ask permission
I miss her—
that carefree spirit
who lived in my skin
before the world taught her
to be careful

who had friends
like scattered stars
making constellations
of ordinary days
sometimes I catch glimpses
of her in mirrors
dancing between
adult responsibilities
and I wonder
if she misses me too
this careful person
I've become
(strange how we can be
homesick for ourselves—
for the people we were
before we learned
how to be grown)

Waiting Dog

We shared endless nights
of play and laughter
you waking me at midnight
me filling your bowl
with sleepy smiles
I was your blanket
against winter winds
your shield when the world
grew too sharp
for your gentle heart
we spoke a language
only best friends know—
made of tail wags and gentle touches
promises neither of us
thought could break
but then came boxes suitcases, tickets
and I became everyone else—
another person who leaves without explanation
now through screens you hear my voice
and search the room with confused eyes
that slowly dim with understanding
I never gave you the goodbye you deserved
no way to tell you why your person
turned to pixels ,
you wait by doors that won't bring me back
 loyal to a promise , I couldn't keep.
(how do you explain airports and oceans
to a heart that measures distance only in
the length of a leash?)

WINGS OF FREEDOM

Your Own Path

Just because others run
doesn't mean your feet
must follow their rhythm
some of us were made
to walk slowly
through flower fields
counting petals
tasting rain,
some of us need
to sit by streams
watching leaves drift
learning life's grammar
at our own pace,
the world may sprint
toward finish lines
but who decided
life was a race?
maybe your journey
is about noticing
what others miss
in their rush
to nowhere
(sometimes victory
isn't about speed
but about choosing
not to race
at all)

Your Waves

Don't tame your tides
for those who prefer
shallow waters
Don't smooth your storms
just because some
like their oceans
postcard-calm
you were born
with the force
of tsunamis
in your blood,
let them seek
their kiddie pools
their safe harbors
their gentle bays,
you are not meant
to be everyone's
swimming lesson
you are ocean—
wild and deep
and beautifully
untamable
(some will fear
your depths
but others will learn
to breathe
beneath your waves)

Like The Moon

Sometimes we are full and bright
lighting entire landscapes
with our silver certainty
but other times
we're just a sliver
of who we used to be
a thin curve of hope
against dark skies
waning, waxing
hiding parts of ourselves
behind earth's shadow
yet even in our darkness
we pull oceans
move tides
affect the rhythm
of entire worlds
you don't need
all your pieces
to be powerful
you don't need
to be complete
to be cosmic.
(the moon never apologizes
for its phases
it just keeps
spinning starlight
from whatever fraction
of itself
it has left)

Wings Need Rest

Even eagles must land
fold their mighty wings
let muscles remember
what stillness feels like
the highest flyers
need earth sometimes
to gather strength
for next horizons
watch how gracefully
they settle on branches
without shame
for needing pause
no bird questions
the wisdom of rest
no wing doubts
its right to fold
so why do we
carry guilt
for our own
necessary landings?
(sometimes the bravest thing
a bird can do
is trust the branch
beneath its feet)

The Birds Above

I was shattered glass
on kitchen floors
counting wrong turns
like copper pennies
devastation wore
my clothes better
than I did
grief knew my name
by heart
I stood at the edge
of giving up
when wisdom found me:
you can't stop
pain's dark birds
from flying overhead
but you can prevent
their nesting
in your hair
and suddenly—
I learned the difference
between visiting pain
and living there
(sometimes freedom
isn't about
stopping the birds
but refusing to become
their home)

Building From Arrows

They wear that smirk
like they own the right
to size my dreams
every time I speak of flight
they try to clip my wings
with practiced doubt
"stay small," they say
not knowing I come from
a place so tiny
it doesn't even know
their bigness exists
they shoot arrows
of mockery and doubt
at every goal I share
not knowing I'm the kind
who builds houses
from others' weapons
they laugh behind my back
in front of my face
at my audacious plans
while I cross oceans
they thought would drown me
let them smirk—
I've learned to turn
their doubt into fuel
their laughter into lift
their arrows into armor
because people who live
in boxes of their own making

will never understand
those of us, who were born
to break through ceilings
(sometimes the greatest victory
is not proving them wrong
but building something beautiful
from all the times
they said you couldn't)

Keep Going

No hammer came with warnings:
"strike just once"
no door whispered:
"knock only today"
no blade insisted:
"cut once, then surrender"
tools know better
than to limit their purpose
roads don't count
how many times
feet stumble forward
your attempts
aren't tallied
by some cosmic
scorekeeper
so keep striking
until the nail yields
keep knocking
until doors open
keep cutting
through obstacles
keep walking
through shadows
let your mistakes
be your teachers
not your limits
(sometimes persistence
is just refusing
to believe in
last chances)

GARDENS OF GROWTH

The Garden

Stop running after
rainbow wings
with desperate nets
and empty jars
instead
plant wildflowers
in your soul
water seeds
of who you're becoming
nurture the soil
of your own growth
let your garden bloom
with authenticity
the butterflies know
where to find
the sweetest nectar
the truest colors
the steadiest stems
they come to those
who grow gardens
not those who chase
with frantic hands
(sometimes attraction
is just patience
dressed in petals)

Seasons of Self

Be gentle with your timeline—
even roses rest
between blooms
the cherry tree
doesn't apologize
for its bare branches, in December
fields don't feel guilty
for their fallow seasons
forests don't rush
their spring awakening everything alive
knows the wisdom
of dormant days
so why do we expect
our souls to flower
without pause?
our hearts to bear fruit
in every season?
let yourself have winters
let yourself lie quiet under snow
trust the rhythm
that runs through
all living things—
bloom will return
when you are ready
(nature never learned to doubt her cycles
perhaps we could learn from her patience)

Trust Again

I could count my betrayals
like battle scars
numbered one to hundred
each a lesson written in pain
yet here I am—
arms open
heart exposed
ready to believe again
call it foolish
call it brave
but I'd rather be
the one who trusted
than the one who
made trust impossible
(some of us are built
to believe in light
even after
a hundred darknesses)

Untold Stories

The story you tell of me, isn't mine—
you speak of obstacles
like they're mountains
but you've never felt
the weight of hunger
keeping midnight company,
you throw stones , in my path
thinking they'll break me
not knowing I've carried
dead dreams on my shoulders
through blizzards,
you talk of difficulty
like you invented pain
but have you ever done
a funeral march uphill, through snow
carrying the corpses, of your hopes?
I've cremated dreams, in lonely cottages
while you spoke
of challenges
like they were games,
you don't know
the story written
in my hollow bones
the epics carved
into my empty stomach
the legends etched
in sleepless eyes
(some struggles are too sacred for those who only
know how to tell other people's stories)

False Faces

Don't ask me what i seek
in someone's heart,
just to wear it
like a borrowed coat
don't study my dreams
like an actor's script
memorizing lines
you'll forget by spring
I've seen too many
method actors
perfect their roles
for opening night
only to drop character
when reviews come in
this isn't theater—
these aren't parts
to audition for
these aren't costumes
you can shed,
my heart isn't staging
for your brief performance
of who you think
I want you to be.
(some roles weren't meant
to be played—
only lived)

Letting Birds Fly

I tried to be the keeper
of other hearts
drew blueprints
for how they should love me
wrote rulebooks
for their affection,
I built cages
of expectations
decorated them
with my needs
called it love
until I learned—
love isn't bars
no matter how golden
isn't wings clipped
to match my comfort
so I opened
all the doors
let them choose
their own flight paths
their own branches
their own sky
because true love
doesn't wear chains
doesn't need locks
doesn't ask permission
to soar

two birds flying free
choosing the same branch
that's the love story
I finally understood
(sometimes loving
means learning
to unlock every cage
we've ever built)

The Beauty of Being Wrong

It's okay to say "I was wrong"—
let the words roll off
your tongue like truth , not stones
there's a certain grace
in admitting mistakes
a strength in showing, your rough edges
your human seams, the need to be right
is a prison of pride
where growth goes, to suffocate
but being wrong?
that's where wisdom, plants its gardens
where better versions, of ourselves take root
so own your errors, like medals of honor
wear your mistakes, like badges that say
"I'm still learning", because perfection
never taught anyone, anything worth knowing
and those who refuse, to bend with being wrong
eventually break, under the weight, of false rightness
(sometimes our finest moments aren't in being right
but in the quiet courage of admitting when we're not)

NEW HORIZONS

My Own Space

I want my own home
not for the freedom
to paint walls wild colors
or dance at midnight,
but for the power
to close doors
on what i don't want to let in,
not for the liberty
to throw parties
or play music loud
but for the right
to choose silence,
not for the chance
to go anywhere
but for permission to stay still
when the world demands movement
not for the ability, to do everything
but for the peace
of doing nothing
when nothing
is what i need,
my own space
where "no"
doesn't need
explanation
where boundaries
aren't negotiations 
(sometimes freedom isn't about what you can do
but what you can refuse to do)

Someday

I keep folding my happiness
into smaller and smaller squares
tucking joy away
for some future shelf
my eyes skip past
sale signs and storefronts
delete emails promising
discounts on dreams
I've become strange
to normal pleasures—
an alien who doesn't speak
the language of shopping carts
and weekend sales
they don't see
how I count pennies
like prayers
how water fills
the spaces
where food should be
all for this promise
I whisper to myself:
someday
someday these wishes
will wake from their sleep
in abandoned carts
someday these wings
will trade water
for first-class clouds

but for now
I keep swallowing
patience like medicine
watching others live
the life I keep
saving for
(how heavy
these dreams become
when we carry them
for too long
without opening)

If I Could Heal The World

If I could be a therapist
I would treat wounds
like precious artifacts
carefully excavating pain
from beneath years of soil
I would open sealed pores
let skin breathe again
like flowers meeting sunlight
for the first time
apply turmeric paste
to yellowing bruises
offer painkillers
like communion wafers
sit through nights
until stories pour out
like cleansing rain
washing away decades
of gathered dust
I would guide each child
through the maze of growing
protect them from thorns
that turn hearts to armor
but these are just dreams
of fixing what's broken
when what i really wish
is to prevent the breaking
because even healed bones
remember their fractures
even mended hearts
carry ghost-scars

even when pain fades
innocence doesn't return
like morning dew
that once disturbed
never forms again
if I could really change things
I wouldn't be the one
who bandages wounds
but the one who stops
the wound from happening
(because some things
once broken
can be fixed
but never return
to their first wholeness—
like trying to put
morning frost
back on a flower)

Where Did I...

I hear their stories flow
like well-rehearsed scripts—
vacation photos, investment portfolios
career ladders climbed, with perfect timing
while I sit here, rewinding my life
frame by frame
searching for the moment
everything tilted wrong
was it that job, I didn't take?
that city I left?
that chance I missed
while counting risks?
I map my mistakes
like a detective
studying cold cases
trying to pinpoint
the exact coordinate
where my path
veered off course
it's not their success
that haunts me
but the ghost of choices
I might have made
I keep searching
for that one wrong turn
as if finding it could give me
a second chance at navigation
(but life isn't GPS— there's no "recalculating route"
when we think we've gone astray)

The Final Leap

When I counted my losses
like empty shelves
in an abandoned store
marked everything off
my inventory of hope
when my pockets held
nothing but lint
and remembered dreams
when even echoes
had packed their bags
and left
that's when I found it—
this strange freedom
in absolute zero
because when you've lost
everything
you finally understand:
the only thing left
to lose
is fear itself
so I spread these wings
made of nothing
but desperate courage
and jumped
(sometimes you need to lose everything
to find the audacity to fly)

Dream Without Limits

Dream so big
it makes others uncomfortable
speak your wishes
into the scared silence
of impossible things
remember:
they once laughed
at the dreamers who said
we'd put metal birds in sky
carrying hundreds
across oceans,
they shook their heads
at the thought of voices
dancing through air
crossing continents
without strings,
they couldn't imagine
memories caught
in pocket-sized boxes
light turned to pixels
time frozen in frames,
who could believe
we'd leave footprints
on moon dust
when we were still
learning to float
in saltwater?
so let them doubt

let them whisper
"impossible"
behind cupped hands
your dreams don't need
their permission
to take flight
because somewhere
in a garage or bedroom
someone is building
tomorrow's impossible
into today's reality
(history belongs
to those who dared
to dream in sizes
that made others
look away)

Breaking Through

Finally, these wings learned to pierce clouds
after years of flying too close to ground,
I push through layers of doubt and fear ,
cotton-thick resistance melting against resolve
up here, above what held me down the sky opens like
a new book
sunlight greets me like an old friend who always knew
I'd make it here
below, my shadows grow smaller, dimmer until
they're just stories I used to believe
now I understand why birds sing— not from habit but
from height
just because clouds hide your sun doesn't mean light
stopped shining
you must rise above these shadows, climb higher than
your doubts can reach
until nothing stands between you and your brightest
possibilities
(sometimes freedom is just the courage to keep
climbing until clouds become stepping stones and the
sun remembers your face)

COMING HOME

The Final Flight Home

The day I book that one-way ticket
my heart will beat like wings
testing freedom for the first time
like a bird whose wounds have healed
ready to soar again, carrying
stories of survival in her feathers
I'll taste this joy like a child's first ice cream
sweet with victory's flavor
the moon will glow brighter
knowing I'm coming home
the sun will polish its rays, just for my return
I'll count seconds in the sky, tick by precious tick
my smile growing wider, with each mile closer
because this isn't just a flight—
it's proof of battles won
medals earned, dreams caught
life finally built strong enough
to carry me back home
back to morning sunshine
and garden chairs
where I'll sit eating guavas
writing poems that taste, like victory
no more distance
no more yearning
just the simple pleasure
of being where
my heart lives
(sometimes the sweetest freedom
is the freedom to finally stay still)

Back to Before

When all these adult wars
are finally won
I'll pack up my victories
and head back home
to mornings spent
standing before wardrobes
drowning in choices
like my younger self
I'll be fashionably late
again, deliciously late
running after buses
that smell like teenage dreams
claiming that same window seat
where I once watched life blur by
without counting costs
or carrying weights
I'll travel that road
between who i became
and who i was—
that carefree girl
who didn't know yet
about life's battles
let me be her again
just for one ride
let me feel that lightness
in my bones
(sometimes growing up
means earning the right
to be young once more)

One Day at the Sea

One day I will stand
where ocean meets earth
let salt water cleanse, my tired feet
my red dress will dance,
with wind's gentle hands
hair finally free, from worry's tight grip
sunlight will paint, diamonds on waves
while I collect moments, like seashells
I'll sit in warm sand
legs folded beneath me
no clock to watch
no time to chase
just me and the shore
sharing stories of survival
whispering to waves:
"look, I made it"
hours will slip by
like grains through fingers
each moment precious
because it's mine to spend
finally free
to waste time
beautifully
completely
(sometimes the greatest
luxury isn't wealth
but the freedom
to sit still and watch waves
without counting minutes)

Dreams of Us

We'll dance through Rome's streets
spin beneath ancient stars,
share candlelit dinners
in Paris nights,
then find ourselves
in cities of snow
where silence falls
soft as promises,
curled together
with coffee steam
and half-read books
on window seats,
watch midnight films
while rain taps glass
like nature's quiet
applause,
bow to each other
on windswept hills
where wildflowers
waltz with breeze,
count moonbeams
in London parks,
measure sunlight
on mountain peaks,
hold hands in airports
between destinations
hearts racing faster
than any plane

we'll paint these cities
with our laughter
color each country
with our joy
running through life
like children through sprinklers
loving each moment
like it's our last
(let's make the world
our living room
every city
our home)

Hold On

Could you please wait?
just a little longer—
I'm working as fast
as dreams can grow
I know time's running
through hourglass fingers
I know change doesn't pause
for those who are gone
but please
hold our place
in this world
like a bookmark
in an unfinished story
don't let go yet
of what we were
of what we'll be
when I return, I promise
when I come back
we'll never need
to say goodbye again
just wait
a little longer
let me finish
building this bridge
back to you
(I'm asking time to be gentle
with what I love until I can
come home to keep it
safe myself)

LIGHT BEARERS

The Song That Saved

Don't ask about my survival
like it's a manual, to be studied
ask instead, about the song
that became my heartbeat
when my own, forgot to pulse
ask about the lyrics
I whispered like prayers, at 3 AM
when breathing
felt like drowning
ask about the melody
that held me together
when everything else
turned to dust
ask about the chorus
that knew my pain
better than my own voice
that promised morning
would come again
ask about the track
worn deep in my playlist
like a path through darkness
leading me home
(sometimes survival
isn't about strength—
it's about finding
the right words
set to perfect music
at the exact moment
you need them most)

Someone Out There

Somewhere in this vast world
someone's day brightens
because your heart beats,
someone smiles
remembering the way
you say hello,
someone feels less alone
knowing you walk
under the same sky,
you may never know
all the lives you've touched
like ripples in still water
spreading outward
touching distant shores,
your existence itself
is a light in someone's window,
a warm cup on their cold days
a reason to believe
in gentler tomorrows
(sometimes we forget
we're all lighthouses
for ships we cannot see
guiding someone home
just by being)

Unplug to Restart

Like tired machines
humming too long
we need our moments
of deliberate darkness,
when screens go black
and circuits cool
when thoughts stop
their endless spinning,
pull your own plug,
let silence seep in
like evening shade
through open windows,
disconnect from
the constant buzz
of being always on,
always available,
rest in your own
soft reboot,
let your system
return to factory settings,
sometimes healing
is as simple as
powering down
before powering up
(funny how humans
and hardware
share the same first aid—
the sacred pause
between off and on)

The Man with the Turban

In the deep of night
when my own troubles
feel too heavy
I see him—
that farmer
unwrapping his turban
with weathered hands
making softness
from dignity
laying his head down
on cloth that carries
prayers and pride
against earth's
hard truths
his face maps
a geography of worry
carved by years
of hoping against hope
not broken enough
to leave
not whole enough
to dream
just steady enough
to stay
for the daughter
who needs schooling
for the wife who believes
for the son too young
to understand

I wish i could find him
beyond this 2 AM vision
that visits when my own path
seems too steep
(sometimes our hardships
send us ghosts
to remind us
we're not the only ones
carrying weight)

Those Who Make Light

Stay close to those
who plant seeds of hope
in your shadowed valleys
who see fertile soil,
where you only felt
barren ground
who know how to tend
gardens in places
you thought too dark
for anything to grow
who carry sunlight
in their pockets
water in their words
spring in their touch
who believe in blooming
even when winter
lives in your bones
who understand that growth
happens first in darkness
beneath the surface
where no one can see
(sometimes love
is just someone
who knows how to garden
in the dark)

Dreamers Don't Clock Out

The heart with dreams
doesn't punch timecards
doesn't watch clocks
doesn't wait for weekends
it works in moonlight
in dawn's first breath
in Sunday silence
in Monday rush
takes quick naps
between possibilities
short breaks, between beliefs
while others live
in scheduled boxes
nine-to-five dreams
lunch-break hopes
this heart beats
to its own rhythm
refuses to sync
with mechanical time
because true dreams
don't know holidays
don't clock overtime
don't take vacations
they just burn
day and night
like stars that never
learned to sleep
(sometimes passion is just rebellion
against the tyranny of timepieces)

Daily Lessons

Life unfolds as classroom—
each sunrise a fresh page
each moment a lesson
waiting to be learned
I collect wisdom
like autumn leaves
store knowledge
like winter stores snow
learning how to breathe
through storms
how to bend, without breaking
how to hold pain
without becoming it
gathering answers
before questions arrive
like squirrels preparing
for seasons yet to come
so when life stops me
with its pop quiz moments
its surprise examinations
of heart and soul
I'll have answers ready
not memorized
but lived through
grown through
earned through time
(sometimes the best
preparation for tomorrow
is paying attention to today)

Unhealed World

We walk these streets
like civilized zombies
briefcases full of deadlines
suits hiding battle scars
each of us carrying
a wounded child inside
swallowing their cries
with morning coffee
we spread our poison
like casual conversation
infecting others
with our unhealed parts
passing trauma
like business cards
teaching new generations
how to bury their light
what if we lined up like broken toys
waiting to be fixed one by one?
what if we opened
these adult shells
and let each inner child
breathe again?
maybe then
this world could heal
from inside out
one rescued soul at a time
(because every war, every hatred, every cruel word
is just another child crying out from behind adult eyes)

Daffodils from Graves

When everything crumbled
to dust and shadow
when hope itself
seemed buried deep
when devastation painted
our world in greys
and grief wrote its name
across our skies
then—
from the graves
of everything we lost
daffodils pushed through
yellow defiance
against darkness
life insisting
on its own rebirth
tender stems
breaking earth's crust
petals unfurling
like new promises
proving that even
in fields of endings
beginnings hide
beneath the soil
(sometimes hope
wears yellow petals
and grows strongest
in places we thought
nothing could survive)